BlackBerry Peach Poetry Prizes 2022

BBP3

BlackBerry Peach Poetry Prizes 2022

Written and Spoken Word Poetry

Sponsored by the National Federation of State Poetry Societies (NFSPS)

ISBN: 9798832780078

Cover photography by Shirley Cavanaugh

Cover and book design by
Gary Broughman, CHB Media

Available on Amazon.com, Barnes and Noble online,
and most online book sellers.

CONTENTS

CONTENTS (continued)

Introduction

The Blackberry Peach Poetry Prizes (BBP3) for written and spoken word poetry, a major national competition sponsored by the National Federation of State Poetry Societies (NFSPS) have been chosen for 2022. The award winning work of the six winners is presented in written and spoken word form (available on the internet via SoundCloud) and in this book.

The winners of this year's BlackBerry Peach Spoken Word Poetry Competition were announced by the Contest Chair, Joe Cavanaugh. First place winner is Wesley Frazier-Keyes of Chicago, Illinois. Second place went to Raymond Jimenez from Orlando, Florida. Third place was awarded to Jessica Temple of Fort Walton Beach, Florida. Honorable mentions went to Kashvi Ramani of Arlington Virginia, Sue Fagalde Lick of South Beach Oregon, and Kevin Campbell (aka Noir Jente) of DeLand, Florida.

This year's competition was judged by Ed Mabrey of Los Angeles, California. He was last year's (2021) BlackBerry Peach Spoken Word Poetry Competition winner and is often considered the top poet in the history of Poetry Slam with four World Championships, five consecutive Regional Championships and over 500 Poetry Slam wins in his career so far. He chose the winners from entries from twelve states, with Florida recording the most entries. Colorado was second for entries, and Oregon was third. Poets were asked to pick their four best poems and submit them in Written and Spoken (audio) form to be eligible for the prizes.

This is the sixth year of the competition and the sixth book published by NFSPS with audio versions available on SoundCloud at www.soundcloud.com/blackberrypeach2022. Videos of the the winners are available on YouTube (2022 BlackBerryPeach Contest Winners).

The tradition of spoken word or performance poetry goes back deep into pre-history. Poetry was performed on stage long before it was captured on the page. Competitive performance poetry was an important part of the Ancient Greek Olympics. With the advent of printing, poetry moved increasingly to the pages of books and into the classroom. Since the 1970s, there has been a resurgence in interest in spoken word and performance poetry, including hiphop (or rap) and slam (which reintroduced competition). Today it is an important cultural mainstay and a favorite among younger poets.

In 2016 NFSPS, primarily a literary organization, established the Blackberry Peach Competition, a major national contest with significant cash prizes to acknowledge and support the value of spoken word poetry.

Many people are responsible for the success of this pioneering endeavor. We thank them all, with special thanks to Shirley BLACKwell, Eleanor BERRY, and Fil PEACH for their help and the commitment of the resources needed to bring written and spoken word poetry together in this annual competition. Special thanks to Gary Broughman and CHB Media for the excellent work creating this year's book, video and poster. Please enjoy the achievements of these talented poets and their prize-winning poetry, presented here in written and spoken word.

Please consider entering the competition in 2023. Contest guidelines are available at www.nfsps.com/BBP3guidlines.html.

Joe Cavanaugh

2022 Blackberry Peach Contest Chairperson

THE WINNING POETS

1ST PLACE PRIZE WINNER

WESLEY FRAZIER~KEYES

WESLEY FRAZIER-KEYES is a native of the south side of Chicago and a proud CPS (Chicago Public Schools) graduate. He has used the art of poetry and spoken word to take him all over the country teaching and competing. He is the 2015 Chicago Grand Slam champion and finished 6th out of 200 poets at the 2015 Southern Fried poetry festival. In 2018 he repeated as Chicago Grand Slam champion and coached the team representing Chicago at the National Poetry Slam. During the 2021 Southern Fried Poetry festival he made another appearance in the finals. Writing and performing became a passion for Wesley at a young age and he cannot wait to see where the creator leads him on his spoken word journey.

SOUTH SIDE

Good morning from the south side!
What day is good for mourning on the south side?
This is how we end summers on the south side.

How we start revolutions on the south side.
How we pray on the south side.
Sons lose mothers in broad daylight.
This is our south side!
We love it!
Can you see our tears?
Can you taste our tears?
But, we don't cry anymore, just mourn.
Our south side.
Our south side.
They say "Wesley you write about Black people too much"
"You write about Chicago too much."
Oh you niggas is silly aint you?
Niggas seem to forget dont you?
Don't worry I'll let this pen remember for you? Remember
Sean
Remember Blair
Remember Derion
Remember Erica
Remember Monee
Do you remember?

I wish I could take their images and stitch them to the back
of your brains so when you sleep
you dream about them.
Wish I could paint their names on your tongues, so when
you speak you are speaking them into
existence.

But you niggas still think that death is pretty.
But they are beautiful. Stars.

We were all stars once and I sent condolences to the family.
But, I can't console her baby boy.
He shivers and shakes through motherless nights.
He spazzes out of his spine.
His very backbone will be strong one day.
He is a God amongst insects.
They stripped him of his Goddess mother.
I'll wrap my arms around him.
Dry his tears with this unworthy poem.
They took his mother away.
Made bullets dance in her heart.
The block is hot again as if it ever cooled.
The block be force feeding me soup.
Taste like blood and broken homes
Like cries and moans.
Like struggle and crush bones.
There are bones in these side walks.
We walk on graveyards daily with Ciroc tombstones and teddy bears.
Oh you didnt that your soul steps secretly on their jawlines.
But this nigga write about the ancestors too much right?
They are we get our strength from to go on.
She is an ancestor now.

Good morning from the south side.
What day is good for mourning on the south side?

GRANNY PIE

No disrespect to anyone Mama, Grandma, Me-Maw, or
Abuela, but Granny's sweet potato pie is
always a hit at the church bake sale.
Got the mothers of the church saying "Hey baby, Uh which
one of these pies did yo grandma
make? Never mind I see it. It's the one with the smile
seeping through the scent of the
cinnamon."
This pie is great migration tested.
Moved from a shotgun shack in MS to an apartment on the
south side.
My Aunite Emma could hear Sam Cooke and his sibling
playing up stairs.
Has found itself sweating over Emmits swollen body.
The funeral, an unfriendly reminder of why when we leave
the south we never go back.
This pie is low end Chicago made
Phillips high school.
7 brothers and 3 sisters.
This pie is pearled out. Too fly.
Looking real regal when she was stepping out to the show.
This pie is a teenage mother in the
50s defying gravity. Bosom baked matriarch. Head of a clan.
A tribe of college graduates and
dope heads.
This pie has Fed a plethora of professionals.
DAMN THIS PIE MUST BE GOOD.
must be perfect in the eyes of the Lord.
Must be tired
Must be strong
Must not cry

Does not cry
Must be immune to tears
This pie

This pie make you wanna make Granny proud.
Had me popping shrooms when I knew I didn't. I want to
make this pie so proud. Be worthy of
every bite.

THE SHOP

My barber is the son of one of the elders at King of Glory
Church of God In Christ.
So it seems fitting that I go to him to fix my crown.
These visit to the throne are not taken lightly.
The barber burden is heavy.
He knows this is more than just a haircut.
Here we heal.
Here we debate deep social issues.
For example, the top 5 basketball players of all time.
Top 5 Rap albums of all time.
Top 5 "anything you can imagine." Gets debated in the shop.
His clients, waiting, chime in the conversation like bells.
He sometimes sings hymns while he cuts and as he finishes
the song and taper all my problems seem to fade.
Where I come from barbers fix more than crooked linings.
They blend art with craft.
Call it therapy.
Back home, shops turn into Switzerland.
Nuetreal zones.
Water holes where the mane of these lines sometimes have
waves.
In the 90s we rocked parts in our head as if our scalps were
the Red Sea.
The shop is where cuts turn into confidence and swagger.
This is for every father stepping up and giving there son his
first hair cut.
This is for the poster on the mirror featuring every haircut
style known to the culture.
This is for seeing yourself in that poster.
This is for the the $7 dollar haircuts from the barber college.
This is for the cacophony of clippers and conversation.

This is for the end. The burning sensation after he wipes the freshly opened skin with alcohol.
This reminds me that beauty is pain

This reminds me that I am alive.
The shop is alive.

CHICAGO BOY

College campuses can't comprehend the backwards bend of my speech.
Saw Buck and Fins.
They say you talk funny Chicago boy.
Why you walking like you got too many graves in your back pocket?
Too many twisted fingers cramping your style.
I heard you from the Windy City.
The hot air from them politicians can be felt blowing from the Gaza Strip to The Gardens (Altgeld Gardens)
Wild wild legends in the making.
Told us tales of sky scarpers rising from the ashes with phoenix steel infrastructures.
I heard you were a Native Son.
Shinnig bigger that those sparking Tommy Guns.
Guts glued to cotton gins.
Disfigured faces and open casket funerals.
As children in Englewood we would crucify milk crates to telephone poles.
Piercing the side of hoops dreams.
In this town, only stones rolled like absent fathers.
Corner stores stood as an oasis of icee cups and pizza slices.
Peeling back Styrofoam cocoons of color.
A brief sabbatical from the summer.
It was hot.
Locked in an eternal dance with the block.
Heartbeat and feet moving to the ballad of bullets based in the brims of fitted caps cocked.
Sirens singing in harmony with homework and poetry.
This is where I learned to give a standing ovation.
On my feet releasing a concerto from my palms.

Clapping for HBO and Mos Def.
Boy don't you know that college, Englewood, and South Shore exist in a crooked triangle.
"You not suppose to be here."
Voices bouncing off my skull.
Soundwaves waving bye to free and reduced lunch.
Waving bye to fried chicken and nachos.
Eating in your lunchroom will always be more nutritious than eating in the café.
As children we would run the sands of Rainbow Beach.
Etching an anecdote of missing pots of gold into the lake.
Why doesn't someone tell these brown boys that there are no riches here.
Nothing but pitchforks and crypts awaiting your corpse.
You stinking up my air.
The smell of Autumn on Chicago blacktops.
Black boys birthed in a garden of 5 stars hugged by a river.
"I want you to get as far away from here as you can."
Run away.
Go Back.
I am just as much warlord as I am housing riot.
Poet and Black Panther.
Sinner and disciple.
In 2000 and whenever my daughter just might walk across someone's stage.
Covered in the dirt that they called us.
Thorns protruding from her side.
Squeeze this rose too tight and you will bleed.

2ND PLACE PRIZE WINNER

RAYMOND JIMENEZ

RAYMOND JIMENEZ is a ceramic artist from the University of Central Florida. He was on team Breaking Bad at the National Poetry Slam in 2016 and was a finalist in the Blackberry Peach Poetry Poetry Prizes in 2019. A facilitator of Orlando Poetry Slam, helping poets find their voices and share their experiences to national audiences, he is currently curator of the Haiku Challenge at the annual Fusion Festival in Orlando Florida.

STUMBLING BLOCKS

I'm not *saying* you're a racist
that would be silly
you're not a "whites only" sign
drippy lead paint on knotted wood
perched above a restaurant door
like a scarecrow for civil rights ...

... No, I'm saying you enjoy the house special
the waitress has already memorized your order
the owner reserves your seat weekly
greets you with a camera shutter wink and cheshire smile
your initials carved into the wood of your favorite booth
memories box stepping down the isles
standing room only so you can't see all the spaces
you're not willing to make for others

I'm not saying you're a bigot
really, I'm not.
you're not a Dodge Challenger with bifurcated bumper
plowing protesters in Charlottesville
exhaust fume breath with two stroke fury
snarling and skidding at the slightest provocation
unyielding as the confederate statue
you refuse to see torn down
no ...

... I'm saying you enjoy the ride
the gas pedal feels plush against your heavy foot
the engine roars like a banshee
makes whispers of shrieking bystanders
that you long to own one, but at a reasonable price,

40% off sticker, or 3/5ths compromise
a fuel injected rush of power
turning radius of a gunshot
everything reduced to speed bumps or green lights
and who needs speed bumps in their lives
wrecking your suspension of disbelief?

I'm not saying you're a nazi
like you're some kind of concentration camp
garbage pit of misery and lost dreams,
the stench of death tinged with bitter almonds and despair
walls of razor wire like bared teeth
the emaciated and forgotten
slipping into the oblivion of your mouth

No ...

... I'm saying you live in an upwind
Subdivision
so you don't have to smell the bodies
That your house is well insulated against the sounds of
family trees snapping
or children begging to be held
but you keep the police on speed dial
in case you spot someone Anne Franking next door.
that some places are built for throwing lives away
and you don't look for them
but you vote for them
and never have to think about
Or concentrate on them again

I'm not saying you're the klansmen or proud boy marching
down the street
a specter for white retribution

I'm saying you're the police escort
you're not the Molotov cocktail thrown into a mosque
you're the starbucks that replaces it
You're not the shooter in a black church
you're the "Buy One Box of Bullets, Get One Happy Meal" sale

I'm not saying you're racist
I'm saying evil only triumphs when good people do nothing
and you're the nothing
What king would call a stumbling block of history

and enough stumbling blocks gathered together
make a wall
or a prison
enough stumbling blocks make a school that can't teach about slavery
enough stumbling blocks make a police force that's never held accountable
make internment camps
and trails of tears
Hundreds of years of stumbling blocks make a nation
a towering mess of rotting parts
unwilling to look at itself

I'm saying the biggest obstacle to justice
isn't evil
it's indifference
it's convenience

I'm not saying you're part of the problem
I'm saying in the equation of life
You're just a benign remainder
In someone else's final solution

SATELLITES

There is a graveyard in the sky

there are stars like phantoms,
though long extinguished
their light still burns from our perspective
each flicker belies a billion years journey
in time and space
from a long dead source
yet, they candle
the last remnants of light continue streaming towards us
as we gaze unaware the root of their brilliance
has long passed

there are satellites
orbiting like a funeral procession
pushed to the outer dark so they can march
with abandon without harming our precious signals
past their shelf lives they wait
for the music to end and their final descent into nothing
to begin

others crash to earth
and become the things
children wish upon mistakenly
believing them to be product of fate
and not obsolescence

there is a cemetery in the ocean
where Jules Vern weeps
and spacecraft are unmade
where the pride of nations rusts
and crumbles

There is an explorer on mars
who sings on their birthday

There is a rocket
(we think from China
but aren't quite sure)
colliding with the moon

There is a dream
unfurling in the sky
it's eyes adjusting to the faintest light
it stretches as we hold our breath
we hope to look deeper and farther
than we have before
to put a mirror to the face of creation

Meanwhile
its predecessor
smiles as it recedes towards oblivion
it's days as being the pinnacle of exploration
now over

This life we lead
is surrounded by decay
and failure

Yesterday's miracles
turned trash heaps
A blip in space leads to catastrophe
A fortune becomes fireworks
in an instant

It is easy to look around
and see only garbage

a world of detritus and missteps
how our every desire
becomes a burden for the next generation
to salvage or discard

In space, your best intentions can stick around
your mistakes become debris you have to navigate
The mess of growth
and yearning
and ambition
become the flotsam of the galaxy

I often wonder what legacy I will leave when I am gone
when I recede into the night
or slip beneath the soil
what remnants of me will remain in orbit
if I have made more waste than I was worth

I find comfort in the notion that I am not alone
that I am in a long line of projectiles hurtling through time
all of us, flying through the vast expanse of the human condition
calculating trajectories
navigating collisions
trying to anticipate the next flare that might send us
cascading downward
hoping not to be relegated to the dark

Maybe stars have it right
maybe all that you can hope for
is that the light you radiate
travels long after you're gone

Maybe obsolescence isn't so bad
if you become a child's dream

Maybe it's all relative, how you can be
both extinguished star
or the light on the other end of the galaxy
just arriving
just becoming a flicker
in someone else's night sky

If I can see it that way,
If I can remember that I am also holding up a mirror
towards creation
That we are all mirrors of creation
unfurling ourselves in the deep
Maybe, I can still remember to dream as well
maybe, I can remember what it's like
to shine

SAY IT *(A response to the Parental Rights in Education Act and the Stop Woke Act in Florida)*

Don't say gay
say straight impaired
say heterosexually challenged
say cisgendered light
say happy
say too friendly
say confused
don't say homophobic
say family friendly
say it like only families are friendly
say it like families can't be gay
like if you're gay you can't be in this family
Don't say pronouns
say my house
say I birthed you and I named you
Don't say homeless
say delinquent
Don't say hate crime
say transpanic
say predator
say get out of my bathroom
go back to your closet
say not in my school
Don't say Alan Turing
Don't say Langston Hughes
Don't say Virginia Wolfe
Don't say Pulse
Don't name them
Don't make them seem human

Also
don't say slavery
say state's rights
say tradition
say heritage
say good people on both sides
Don't say reparations
Don't say woke
Don't be woke
Don't act woke
unless you're joking about how woke someone is
don't say critical race
say, "I don't see race"
Don't say affirmative action
say merit based pay

And please don't say the names
Don't say Trayvon
Don't say Amir
Don't say Castille
Don't talk about not being able to breathe
the long list of names
that keeps getting longer
it will be seasons before you finish speaking
Don't say protests
say riots
talk about Martin Luther King
but only to end the conversation
Use him like a bullet from a balcony to kill uncomfortable discussions
that white people don't want to have
Don't say white people
Say patriots

Don't say racism
but say reverse racism
As much as you possibly can
say you won't be replaced
say my potato salad is seasoned just fine
say, this is my country
say, pick yourselves up by your bootstraps
Don't say indoctrination
say history
Don't say defund public schools
say my child my choice
Don't say slavery
Don't say gay
Don't say Genocide
or internment camp
or forced marches

Don't teach accountability
Don't say problematic
Don't say systemic

Don't talk about the things
a country is embarrassed of
Don't tell the story of America
as though we weren't always heroes
as if every part of us isn't star spangling awesome

Don't break the spell
Don't cast the magic
that goes straight to the bones
Don't make us see it
Don't make us rip open the storybook
and find the blood between the pages
Don't unearth all the happily ever afters that never came

Don’t let the children know
there’s more to the tale than what we’re telling
how fairy godmother’s don’t come to everyone
and how princes, like governors, aren’t always charming
how the world isn’t built by magic
but by decisions
from flawed people
who refuse to admit they were wrong
or that they benefit from living in the embers of tragedy

Don’t tell them how words have power
to recognize
to inspire
to create
to change the very pages of the storybook into something
better than magic
to something real
that you can actually see

Don’t say it
because if you do
they might believe that they are part of the story too
and they might start writing the next part themselves.

TELLING TIME

When he hits you
they will say he snapped
but it will sound like
you are the one breaking

When he hits you
you will wonder if
your cheeks were always
gasoline
and his palms
always lit matches

When he hits you
he will seem a geyser
gushing steam
boiling heat and granite rage
a geological event
beyond a five-year-old's grasp

When he hits you
you will be relieved
you no longer
have to spy on clocks
to measure the distance
between you
and the next eruption
remember that he
is the clock
and it is now
striking you

When he hits you
you will not cry tears
but brass fittings and gears
you will shudder, stutter, click
he instance will be carved inside the back of your skull like a maker's mark
you will sway like a pendulum
you will never be the same again

When he hits
You will not understand gravity
or acceleration
or the physics of collision and motion
but you will obey their gospel
and you will fall like
hourglass sand
spilling into nothing

When he hits you
you will blame yourself
because it wouldn't happen
if you didn't deserve it
because father's
only hit their sons
when they deserve it
you just don't know why
you deserve it so much

But when he stops hitting you…

… you will love him because he's your father
you will love him because you need to love him
you will love him because you need to believe it is over

even though you know it isn't
even though he's promised this so many times before

when he stops hitting you
you will no longer spy on clocks
to measure the distance between you
and the next eruption
you will no longer
smell the coming rainstorm and know it is rumbling for you
you will believe him when he says he is sorry
you will forgive him
as easily as falling from gravity

but when he stops hitting you
you still listen for the clocks in other people
you will watch their faces like minute hands
your feet will tense in anticipation of shifting earth
the hair on the back of your neck nervous
from every chilled wind promising a thunderstorm
you will look for vapors of gasoline in blank stares
and watch for the dirt rising up to meet you

When he stops hitting you
you will promise yourself to never be the victim
you will promise yourself to never become sand
you will swing like a pendulum
You will smash that clock before
it ever has the chance

When you hit him
this stranger who is not your father
this person who
is made of loose fittings and broken gears

you will feel the click as your knuckles fit into place
you will speak only in thunder and matches
you will pray for his sand to spill out

When you hit him
the collision will be like a memory in reverse
you will hear the sound of snapping
you won't care how the universe rotates back
into the same position it was before
all you know
all you understand
is that you are now the clock
and you know what time it is.

3RD PLACE PRIZE WINNER

JESSICA TEMPLE

Photo by TC Caldwell

JESSICA TEMPLE earned her PhD in poetry from Georgia State University and teaches at Northwest Florida State College. She attended the 2019 Sewanee Writers' Conference as a contributing participant in poetry and was named Alabama State Poetry Society's 2019 Poet of the Year. Her work has recently appeared in *Wraparound South; Crab Orchard Review; Canyon Voices*; and *Stone, River, Sky: An Anthology of Georgia Poems* from Negative Capability Press, among others. She is the author of *Daughters of Bone* (Madville Publishing, 2021) and *Seamless and Other Legends* (Finishing Line Press, 2013). Find out more at jessicatemple.com.

PRAISE THESE KIDS

Praise the ear buds
that don't quite dampen the sounds.
The iPhones catching it all
for the record. The backpacks,
their only armor.

Praise the tears,
their fear and their fearlessness,
the shaking hands and snotty noses,
the corners they huddle in.

Praise their voices that refuse,
now, to be silenced.

Praise the teachers, who never asked for this,
who, too, are terrified, who nonetheless
add *human shield* to their resumes.

Praise the polycarbonate
and Kevlar protecting the team
that eventually sweeps the school.

Praise the bullets that fall
harmlessly in hallways,
that do not find purchase
in lungs or liver.

Praise the half-staff flags
flying as reminder.
But do not praise the gunman,
nor the guns.

Never praise the guns.

LEMONADE IN ELEVEN CHAPTERS
(after Beyoncé)

Intuition go with the gut
that gut got magic

Denial this where you end up
when that gut talk
and you ain't listen

Anger what you got when you realize
yo gut had it right all along
you angry with him,
the situation, yo gut, an yoself

Apathy when you get tired of being angry
when you just get tired

Emptiness you feel like you lost everything you ever had
but you ain't
you lost something, yeah, but there's plenty left
you just got to find it

Accountability you know it ain't all his fault
you had your hand in it too

Reformation some lessons you got to learn the hard way

Forgiveness you might as well go on and show him
some mercy
have some mercy on yoself too

Resurrection when things settle down
you got a life to get back to
or a new one to get started

Hope sometime it feel like you ain't got none
sometime that all you got

Redemption sometime you got to save somebody
sometime that somebody is you

THE DONOR

Now I am nervous, bordering on scared
I've never been so pricked/prodded/invaded
I half-believe they will find something unexpected
Some buried tumor or cyst that will change my course
And because I half-believe, it will not be unexpected
With such a family history could it ever be wholly
unexpected

Now my veins go warm as I slide in and out of the tube
Focus on the ceiling/the flowers/the butterflies painted on
the tiles
Taste the metal, hold my breath while the lights change

Now I eat two dinners because I couldn't decide and
I probably won't eat for the next few days anyway
Now I ask for extra towels in the hotel room
Now I remove all my jewelry
Now I shower with the Hibiclens
Now I sleep

Now I wake at 4 and again shower with the Hibiclens
It is thick/sticky/syrupy

Now we are driving
Now in a dark waiting room on the fourth floor
Now I am in a purple party gown and no-slip socks
Now I sign a form
Now I am rolling down a hallway
Now I am awed by the size of the O.R. and talk to a nurse

Now my body is a balloon

Now I float back into my body
Now I am both asleep and awake
There is pain but also not pain
There is sound and not sound
There are voices that are not voices
My eyes are closed or they are open
I am still floating, but I am floating in my body now

Now my kidney is in a cooler on a plane to New York
And I hold a nurse's hand and cry
The pain team shoots nerve blocks into my abdomen
Two or three more holes
I've lost count
Again I am awake/asleep

Now I am rolling through another hallway
I see the pre-op nurse and call to her
Everything went great/I feel fine

Now I ask for orange juice with the Miralax
Now I cry as I vomit orange juice and bile
Now I rest

Now it stings as she clears the line with saline
Pushes more medication in

Now the pain in my chest and shoulders is nearly unbearable
My face, now, is the face of 10 but the most I'll say is 4

Now I am up and walking
Now I am dressed in my own clothes
Now I am riding down in an elevator

Now I am in the car crossing the river and the mountain and
Now I am home

I am pulling myself up
I am showering carefully
I am not touching the incision
I am wearing comfortable clothing
I am drinking GoodBelly mango juice
I am keeping the pillow between me and the seatbelt
I am walking the dog slowly with the waist leash so he
cannot pull too much

Now I rub vitamin E gel onto my scar
Now I write a postcard to the recipient
Now I wait

ELEGY

It is both easier and harder than I expected.
Knowing, as we all do, that it is time,
there are no questions, no explanations needed.
Just some words of reassurance,
a shaved leg, and three small syringes.
Her little heart is beating so fast I say
and then it's not, her body—now just a body—
limp in my lap. Her eyes do not close
and the life does not leave them,
bright as ever, though a nudge of her head
brings no response.

An hour later I begin the digging,
rocks and red dirt no match for my heartbreak.
Down and down I think.
I think of Seamus Heaney and that 4-foot box
(though that's a different poem),
and I'm glad there's no blooming bruise
on her tiny temple, her small body still perfect outside,
though wrecked inside as she weakened.

The last cat I buried was twenty years ago,
hit by a car in front of our driveway.
That was so different. The rough, lolling tongue,
loose as a boat unmoored in his mouth.
The shock of white bone protruding cleanly
through black matted fur.
In my memory, he was stiff when I lifted him from asphalt,
placed him in the cardboard box on the floorboard.
Dug a hole not ten feet from this one.

Now, the digging done, I go to get my girl.
Taking her from the carrier, I prepare for the worst.
They've put down a pad
since bodies can evacuate themselves,
but it's still dry and clean, her body too tired even for this.
I scoop her up in the thin pillowcase she's wrapped in,
not wanting to see her now.
Her body's still warm against my belly,
and I stupidly want to check for breathing.

When it's all done, I haul two flat pavers
from the edge of the garage to mark the spot
and keep the coyotes from digging her up.
I stand for a moment to catch my breath.
The December wind is cold and angry.

HONORABLE MENTION

KASHVI RAMANI

KASHVI RAMANI is a sophomore in high school, pursuing a Film Studies and Entrepreneurship dual enrollment program at two separate schools. Her roots in writing began at six years old but specifically branched as a poet closely before being elected to the 2020-2021 DC Youth Slam Poetry Team. Most recently, she was selected as the 2022 Arlington County Youth Poet Laureate, being one of two of the first Indian-American YPLs in the area. Her pieces have been published in Brown Girl Magazine and Rattle, as well as been recognized by Scholastic Art and Writing Awards, Young Poets in the Community, Collaborative Solutions for Communities, Poetry Society of Virginia, and more. She was a 2022 Young Arts National Finalist in Spoken Theatre and National Merit award winner in Spoken Word Poetry as well! She hopes to offer a unique perspective with her work as a young female Indian-American and make a difference in her own small way.

MY *DODDA* IN A DAY

When the clouds part, my grandmother is on the move. Her locks
flap in the wind, she hides the flaps on her skin. She always finds
a way to burrow inside herself, to position her limbs
in the shadows of the sun. She runs faster each time reality
catches up.

India rises from its trout-lipped slumber and her basket
is already filled with buds. Jasmine sugarcoats her
already-strained smile (she'll have to fix that by noon) and prepares
to string itself on garlands. *Dodda* works its milky color to a lather
and scrubs until a bumpy rash of rose envelops
her brown. Not cream; she will try again tomorrow.

At 11, she bustles down flights of stairs, kneading dough
until the salt that drips from her face is enough
seasoning, until the blood that washes over her hands
hides the henna, flavors dough with *sindoor.* So she sweeps
a mark across her forehead and prays. Clasps her
hands, asks for a new face.

The clock finally chimes 12 and she dons four *tiffins* of lunch
and a crimson *sari* to wash out the weakness. Her feet are
quick. Her husband's are quicker. When he's through,
her wavering teeth—more ocean than stronghold—attack

her own hands over and over and recrudesce
in waves over and over and-

3 PM and she practices teetering spoons on her palms
to prepare for the weight of the world on her shoulders. Her
daughter-in-law is growing grayer and frailer (men like
a little meat on the bones—more cooking for *Dodda*). Her
niece, who once painted the solar system on her eyelids, let her
planets get lost on earth (the ones who aren't pretty need
to be smart —*Dodda* can't marry them off right away). And her
daughter who runs at the same time as she does every morning
to connect with the life she once had (she shuffles through

a gated neighborhood in neon Adidas while *Dodda* turns around
to watch for hungry eyes in sandals that peel at the heels).

The nightjar sings in tune with her landline. Quiet, subliminal
darkness unfolds the cloak of nighttime. 13,000 miles
away we are greeting the sun. We prattle about carnivals
and tank tops, about new friends and opportunities, about
technology, about goals. "*Dodda*, when will you come to see us?"
"Soon, *bungaru*, soon." Then she tucks her-
self in with a blanket that steams like rice and dreams
her wishes into our
realities.

INDIAN REPRESENTATION

I never learned a second language.
Amma would holler in a foreign tongue
Words swirling around in confusion
Bitter to taste at first,
Until I remember the familiar flavor
A phrase finally memorized after years of practice.

Second grade, new school.
Eyebrows furrowed at the large white exterior
Powdering the front of the school.
Daunting
Unfamiliar
My classmates
Color of the school.

Gaze drifts to the brown sheep at the back
In stark contrast to pearly white.
The mean ones tease my food and frizz
The nice ones ask what country I'm from,
And cock their heads when I recite the Pledge of Allegiance.

I run when I see him.
They ask if we are related
Replacing questions with rumors of marriage
But only when I come of age.

When I near him in the hall
I sprint from my past;
From the language I never knew
From my dad's animated fingers painting stories of gods
From the colored packets containing magic
Our own version of Holy
But with an "I."

I can't be both.

The dash permanently
Erased from my life.
My two worlds
Like words in a series
Indian, comma, American.

THE NEWS

The news came mixed in brownie batter.
In the oil of garlic knots, sizzling at the touch.
Tossed in the salad like secrets two years old,
Tucked in the caramelized sunset orange of a Hi-C,
Coated with an extra layer of bubbles as protection.

My ninth birthday was all giggles and giddiness;
My family by my side, arcade coins itching to be cashed in in my pocket,
My favorite restaurant.

A glance to my mom,
And my heart shriveled to a nectarine pit,
Dropped to the pits of my stomach.
"Marrow," "Two weeks," "Incurable."
I haven't been to the restaurant since.

My heart stayed solitary all through winter.
No food to accompany it; I picked at my plate.
His departures cycled with the seasons,
Cycled without reason.
He was gone for three months once.
When we heard a faint rap at the door, my eyes lit up like Christmas lights.
He left the next week, taking my mother with him.
"Your sister needs you to be brave."
So I was.

They always presume two years older than I am.
The familiar surprise laced with disdain.
The six letter word they call me far too often-
"Mature" is too familiar a frequency,
But "mature" is just "suffer" smothered.
"Grown-up" trails out before "too fast" can speak.

Even burns out.
It might be seasoned with a little determination
And garnished with a three stems of hope,
But nothing lasts forever,
So in place I wrote a letter.

"Dear Ramani", it starts
(not Dad - mature means first name basis).
I wish you told me before you did.
I wish you wouldn't carry the storm clouds
with shaky hands,
And fingers that freeze over with emptied pill bottles.
I wish your once glinting smile of promises wasn't crumpled
in the pages of hospital bills.

I wish mine didn't crumple along with yours.
I wish the leaves didn't fall when you leave.
Even when you're here, you're gone;
When you're gone, I wish I didn't have to worry you'd be
gone forever,
I wish that 10 years wasn't tacked on to maximum.
I wish it was out with the "in" in incurable.
I wish Gold could Stay.
I wish I was eight again;
The time before war was slipped under my door
Before "suffer" merged with "mature".

WOMAN REDEFINED

-no, but a young Woman can be criticized for anything She
does.
wears a little makeup to make Herself feel good
(no, don't cake your face and fool the boys).
cries when She's had enough
(no, your life is perfect, pain undeserved).
tries in school
(no, boys don't like them smart),
acts a fool
(no, all Girls are the same).
"No"
stops stinging, the word's frequency now a dull throb.
but when She's terrified,
knows this isn't what She wants,
"no" doesn't roll off the tongue.
gets stuck in Her throat. leaves Her feeling the broken She
knows they call her.
but no, forget it happened, no,
it's Her fault.

18th century made evolution, no, revolution, no,
condemnation
of fabric of country.
founding fathers preach new ideas with a blind eye to
Women suffrage,
no, to slavery,
no, to peace and prosperity.
why do we let a country created by men, now run by men,
no,
ruined by men,
ruin once again? teetering laws are arguing parents-
"no, honey let the grown-ups talk".
they decide our fates like karma,
force fingers to our lips and silence our cries.

our hands itch to push back,
but no,
a "good Girl" rests hands in laps.
even when they strip us of all liberties.
make us more bone, no, more object, than Woman,
the blame of their actions still weigh on us like a storm cloud
that
never.
stops.
pouring.

so we carry the weight of the world on our shoulders,
know that men will claim the burden is left to them.
no, but we agree with tight-lipped smiles and teary eyes
as another woman preaches "boys will be boys".
and the cycle continues.

no. ignoring the problem won't make it go away.
no. we can't sit back and watch as Her beauty is taken, no,
ripped,
and Her joy with it.
no. don't succumb to the sword they brandish over and
over, no,
we've always been the better fighters.
because we've
never.
stopped.
fighting.

break the cycle with the hands you were told to keep gentle
break tradition, break submission,
redefine "Woman".

HONORABLE MENTION

SUE FAGALDE LICK

SUE FAGALDE LICK, who lives in Newport, OR, has published two chapbooks, *Gravel Road Ahead* and *The Widow at the Piano: Poems by a Distracted Catholic*. Her poems have appeared in *Rattle, The MacGuffin, Willawaw, Cloudbank, New Letters, The American Journal of Poetry*, and other publications. She returned to poetry after many years working as a journalist in the Bay Area, earning her MFA in creative writing at Antioch University Los Angeles at age 51. When not writing, she is a music minister and president of the Oregon Poetry Association.

LIFE SENTENCE

He's pissed. When the nurse says, again,
"Honey, you've got to eat," he explodes.
"Stop telling me what to do! I'm not hungry."
He knocks her hand off his shoulder, her brown
hand with perfect pink nails, and he wheels away,
best he can with a fat bandage smashing his fingers
into a stiff red paw. It's her doing, all of it.
She likes to boss people around, this Filipina
overseer of the nursing home in the crumbling convent.
Patients live in the nuns' old cells. That's what they are,
prison cells. He's getting out as soon as he can walk.
Enough of these girls pushing him around, enough
of the crap they call food, enough of his kids
spending money he saved all his ninety-seven years.
For what? Band-Aids and watery oatmeal, a mattress so thin
he can't roll over in the night. He's in jail, having
committed no crime except to live so damn long
his legs gave out. Now his arm is swollen
twice its normal size. It's their fault, the girls
who move him, digging their nails in.
Elevate it on this pillow, they say. To hell with that.
He throws the pillow at a potted plant,
telephones his son. "Get me out. Right now."
He waits in his borrowed wheelchair,
toothpaste on his tennis shoes, soup on his shirt.
Someone hollers for help. High heels slap linoleum.
The warden is on her way. If only he could run.

HOSPICE

I've spent days, months, aching years
pacing the halls of hospitals and nursing homes.
You sleep more than you wake, sometimes so deep
I pray your chest still rises and falls.
Don't die. I have grown so used to being here,
my place this chair beside your bed or in the halls
tracking down nurses to clean you, turn you,
feed you, or calm my fears. Are those numbers
blinking on the screen anything to worry about?
Should you be breathing like that? *Don't die.*
In room after room, other daughters and wives
sit in their plastic chairs between runs for help,
sending texts to the others still living other lives.
We memorize the shift changes: when the Indian nurse
changes places with the one from Mexico,
when the doctor who cares comes hurrying in.
For days, for months, for endless years, we wait,
standing occasionally to stretch, look out the window
at traffic gathering on the streets below, vaguely
remembering when that used to be our lives.
Don't die. I study your face, your shuttered eyes,
the rising and falling of your chest. I hold your hand,
still warm. *Don't die.* Don't force me to walk away,
to take the elevator all the way down
to a world I no longer understand.

AMERICAN PRIMITIVE

I'm trying not to be embarrassed.
My father's new caregiver,
a handsome man from Africa,
leaves his shoes at the door,
as if the matted-down high-low
that crunches with cracker crumbs
could be harmed by a little more dirt,
as if the stained-gold linoleum
patched with yellow tape won't
dirty his designer socks.

It's 80 degrees in here.
"Where's the AC?" he asks.
My father, sitting on a pile
of rank blankets and pillows,
foldup walker at his side,
points to the standup fan. "There."
"No, it's too hot. Where's the AC?"

I follow him into the kitchen,
where dishes are washed in a pan,
the hot water faucet hangs backwards,
and the refrigerator roars,
its sticky shelves holding only
ketchup packs and yellow cheese
gone to rubber months ago.

"Do you have any plastic gloves?"
he asks. My father, nearly deaf,
squints, struggling to hear.
"What? Speak louder."

"Plastic gloves!" "What for?"
As I move my luggage out,
I chuckle to myself.
Wait till he sees the bathroom.

SORROW IN EVERY BED

As I say goodbye, my father sobs.
I make it to the stairwell before
sorrow rips me open like massive
hands pulling out my guts,
splatting them onto the pier like
the innards of a halibut
while a sea gull waits to pounce.

I take what's left of me
to the car, lock the doors,
keen until the cell phone rings,
my brother needing an update.
"I can't stop crying," I say.
I can still feel his bony
shoulders as I held him,
as I promised to come back.

My brother, shake in his voice,
tells me to "hang in there."
How could I leave him here,
naked under his flowered gown,
diaper full of shit, tubes
in his penis, ribs, nose,
nothing left but a red button
to which no one responds?

I'm all he has left, but I need
to go back to a life where
people wear clothes and walk
on strong legs in good shoes.

I need to log back in
to my house, dog, work.
I need to eat in a restaurant
where no one chokes,
screams for help, or dies.

I tear myself away, but
where can I go from here,
now that my guts lie rotting
next to the corpse of a halibut,
sea gull pecking my heart?
Slowly, I put my car in gear,
merge into the line of drivers
going home on a regular day.

HONORABLE MENTION

KEVIN W. CAMPBELL

(NOIR JENTE)

KEVIN W. CAMPBELL (aka NoirJente) is a resident of DeLand, FL by way of the Bronx, NY. He is an accomplished writer, poet and spoken word artist. He has been published in numerous anthologies and literary journals and is the author of the chapbook, *Sadoto* (2014). Mr. Campbell has served as Slam Coordinator of Mainstreet Art and Culture Slam of DeLand since 2014, and has served as Slam Coordinator of both the Florida State Poets Association and the Creative Happiness Institute since 2015. In his work as slam coordinator, he has helped facilitate the dreams of countless poets and writers in representing DeLand and Central Florida in over two dozen regional and national poetry competitions and festivals. Mr. Campbell is an activist and works closely with the board of directors of the African-American Museum of Arts of DeLand.

LETTER FROM AN ABSENTEE FATHER

Dear son,

I didn't see you today cause your momma felt it would be better that way-not necessarily for me or for you, but definitely for her- so what's a father to do? I'm writing this letter though I know you won't receive it; yeah, I gotta put this down now so later you'll believe it. Perhaps one day, when this all calms down, your wonderful smile will replace that frown I saw when your mother kept us apart- son, please believe it just broke my heart.

To properly tell this tale of no one winning, it's probably best to start at the beginning. Truth is, your mother and I were only friends. Love never had a chance, just the lust, then just the end. But, nine months after our passion had abated, the two of us had to deal with the life we created. Now, I had offered to make an honest woman of your mom, but she called me a scrub and laughed at my job. An honest day's work for an honest day's wage was not her idea of a man getting paid. Now, that didn't stop her from going to court and having them award her child support. Not that I mind 'cause you're worth every cent, I'm just not sure how the money's being spent. Your momma's got coach bags and bling like Dr. Dre while you're sportin' K-mart gear that's seen better days. Then, she started running with your "uncle" Pete, who is no kin to you and sells rocks on the street. I guess her idea of livin' large has prevailed, even though at times it means someone ends up in jail. Remember those "vacations" you spent at my house? Those were the times neither one could bail out. Through it all, I loved you the best I knew how to and tried to show you right versus the wrong you're exposed to.

When I came over today to pick you up, your moms said she was broke and tried to hit me up. The lights were on with plenty of food in the house, so I asked her "what for?" 'cause I had my doubts. She said she needed cash 'cause Pete was in jail, and he had major problems if he couldn't post bail. He was in under the alias of Howard Pike, 'cause Peter Trout had two prior strikes. "Not my problem" I said to your mother. "I'm responsible for my son, not his moms, and not her lover". Besides, I never liked all them drugs 'round my kid, so I give less than a damn 'bout Pete's 20-year bid. I suggested she get with his other girlfriends, and maybe between the four of them they could scrape up the ends. No sooner had that last escaped my lips, your momma straight went off, really started to trip. Guess she didn't know Pete had other ladies, but what did she expect from a dude that shady? Anyhow, that's why she's mad, that's why she slammed the door, that's the whole reason I don't see you anymore. But rest assured one day we'll see each other again, even if I have to sue for custody as the means to that end. Until then, chin up little warrior and please don't be sad. Just remember the things I've taught you . . .

Love,

Dad

AMERICA KILLS ME

America kills me with her kindness,
her offers of a cruise, a job, and shelter
that my ancestors just could not refuse.
America kills me like some psycho frenemy,
always doing me dirty then wondering why
I ain't trying to mess with her no more.
America kills me with her generosity,
her endless buffet of hot and cold wars
that fill up morgues and leave ghettos empty.
America kills me like too much rat poison in my skag-
while I take a fix so I can forget all about her,
she is fixing it so she can forget all about me.
America kills me with her red lines,
how moving on up is just for tv shows.

Lady Liberty,
why you front like you got class,
but playin' all us?
Hey there Uncle Sam,
how come you say you want me,
but your borders closed?
Dear America,
why you tellin' me I'm free
but still got me chained?

America kills me like a vampire with Ebola
one way or another, she'll get the job done.
America kills me with her ratrace,
how her last hired, first fired
means I'm always looking for work.
America kills me like a street corner 40 ounce,

passes me around, consumes every last drop,
then leaves me on the concrete in little pieces.
America kills me with her Justice,
how she sees my existence as a crime,
yet stays blind to my pleas for equal treatment.
America kills me like the 13th Amendment is Lucy,
and my fight for freedom is Charlie Brown-
and hell no he ain't kicked that football yet.

AFTERMATH

We aren't talking.

I could write something cute,
write about ships
passing in the night,
about calm seas,
about treacherous waves,
about shipwrecks.

Or maybe
how many months and weeks
it's been,
be Prince, be Sinead,
count down
the hours and days,
tell just how deep
the time has nosedived.

But,
I've lost count
of the all the summers
I've spent beached.
I can't recall how long
it's been since…We.
And,
that's not the point.

We aren't talking.

I'm sure
I can point as many fingers

as you can.
I'm sure
we can both pinpoint
exactly when love died.
I'm sure
we would not point out
the same moment.

I felt you
move away long before
we said goodbye.
I bet
at least on that
we'd agree.

I know
you'd want this
to be about you
but,
I just now realized
I've piloted this ghost ship
for much longer than
I first thought.

All you did
was climb aboard,
raise a toast,
Pretend
to lay on,
to fasten a knot,
to sing shanties,
to … walk a plank.

We aren't talking.

No matter how much
I'd love to be
eternally in Spring
I know full well
some things
will always be born
to live and die
completely in Winter.

No matter how much
we tried to keep
each other warm,
our efforts were futile,
foolish folly bound to succumb
to frigid waste,
to the mountains of ice
we'd spent lifetimes forming.
No ship has ever survived
between two icebergs.
perhaps we should have known…

We aren't talking.

Sometimes
you can sail
seven seas laughing
hard in every port
yet still never
land home.

Sometimes "for a season" vs.

"for a reason" vs.
"for a lifetime" is
complete and utter nonsense.

Sometimes
you can get everything right
and still fail miserably.
Sometimes
you discover you've been asking
the wrong questions.

We aren't talking.

Yet
here we are
at the end of the world
with Death peeking in
through both our windows.
Here I am,
at last with the right questions,
yet dreading to ask,
yet hoping for answers,
unsure I want
to say or hear either.

Here I am
with my finger poised over a button,
with Death outside my door,
sitting with my pride,
and my need, and myself…
and wondering which of us three
will die first.

THE GOD THAT BE BLESSIN' 'MURICA

All this time I been expectin' too much of you, 'Murica.
All this time I been wrong for thinkin' it's your fault.

But I just realized you can't help it.
You wasn't born bad, though you might as well have been.

It's your God that screws you up.
Your homicidal, genocidal, date raping God.

What did Mary know and when did she know it?
Did she dress provocatively, was she asking for it?

Maybe God just waited 'til she passed out from too much wine.
Too much Jesus Juice, and HE swooped in to divinely have HIS way.

God be the best cat burglar rapist of all times.
HE be smooth with HIS, just ask Dr. Huxtable.

It's your God that screws you up.
Your fornicating, woman stealing, one-night stand God.

I wonder how it really was when Joseph found out.
It ain't like he could do a damned thing about it no how.

God didn't even have the decency to tell him HISSELF.
Sent one of those angel thugs to do HIS dirty work.

Bet it went down like an episode of Maury- YOU ARE NOT THE FATHER!

Bet Joseph was the one who invented the phrase "deadbeat dad".

But it ain't like Joseph was gonna work up the nerve to step to God.
First and last time someone tried it they ended up in Hell, the Devil know.

It's your God that screws you up, 'Murica.
Your half stepping, voyeuristic, schizophrenic God.

HE that blesses so well you can afford to spread damnation.
HIM so closely conjured in your image you feel comfortable destroying truth.

How much you wanna bet their Allah and your I AM be the same dude?
Lay a hunnert that Jesus and Muhammed got the same fingerprints!

I can hear HIM laughing when Christian hates Muslim
white hates black, man hates woman, cis hates queer,

I can hear HIM chuckling, tinkled the same pink you are snickering at the irony of HIS promise to redeem you all with THE BLOOD.

HE knew you'd never read the fine print.
HE knew you'd never figure out the blood would be yours.

JUDGE

ED MABREY

ED MABREY, actor, author, and speaker, exemplifies the modern-day renaissance artist. From the page to the stage and the script to the screen, Ed captivates, motivates, and promulgates the performing arts. He is considered the greatest poet in the history of Poetry Slam—four World Championships, five consecutive Regional Championships, and over 500 wins in his career. Ed tours the country professionally as a poet, comedian, and professional speaker. Also, an NAACP Image Award Nominee, Ed has been on Seasons 3, 5, and 6 of *Verses and Flow* (TV One), as well as appearing on broadcasts on ABC, FOX, HBO All Def Digital, Crackle, CNN, and C-SPAN. Ed was a speaker at 2015 TEDx Dayton and 2017 TEDx Evans Street. As the 2019 APCA Spoken Word Artist of the Year, Ed has performed at over 200 colleges and universities around the country, teaching workshops and conducting seminars. A Watering Hole graduate fellow and Scioto Retreat Cohort, Ed is a Pushcart nominee and contributed poems to a New York Times National bestselling anthology.

BBP3 Chair & Managing Editor: Joe Cavanaugh

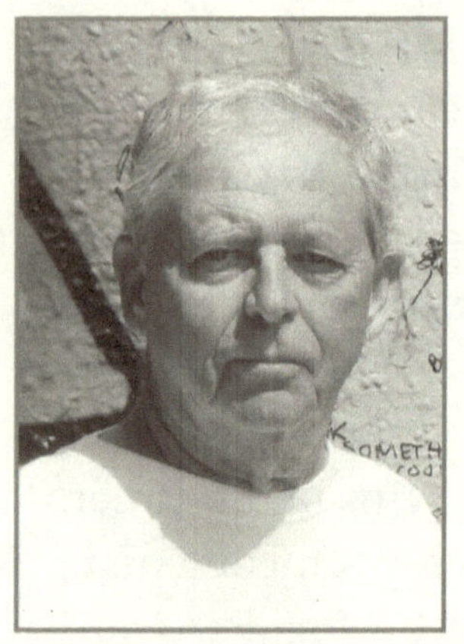

Joe Cavanaugh began his career by accepting President Kennedy's challenge to help build a better world by serving in the Peace Corps. He is the author of four poetry books, *Poetry Jam with Toast and Tea, California Dreamin, Love Happens A Target on my Chest,,* and *Transcendental Targets, Searching for the Ecstatic in a Cloud of White Butterflies.* He served as President of the Florida State Poets Association for four years and is currently a Vice President of the National Federation of State Poetry Societies. He is a 2016 recipient of the Creative Happiness Institute's Community Service Award for his volunteer service to poetry and the greater community. He is the first and current Chairmen of the BlackBerry Peach Poetry Prizes. He lives in Ormond Beach, Florida, and is a member of the Daytona Live Poets. His latest book, *The Poet and the Wondersmith,* is available on Amazon. Visit www.josephcavanaughpoet.com.

BBP3 Media Editor: Gary Broughman

Gary Broughman is publisher at CHB Media, an Indie press which has edited, designed, and published more than 85 titles since 2009, including many volumes of poetry. Gary is the editor of the Florida State Poets Association's annual anthology, *Cadence.* He also is president of Positively Florida, a 501(c)(3) nonprofit which supports "arts and ideas to feed the spirit." Among other activities, Positively Florida produces live theater in Central Florida, teaches creative writing classes and facilitates sessions of the Julia Cameron program, *The Artist's Way*. Gary is active in the writing arts as a poet and novelist, and in the performing arts as an actor, director, and producer. Inquire about publishing services at ***chbmedia@gmail.com***, at www.*chbbooks.com*, or call 386-957-4761.

www.ingramcontent.com/pod-product-compliance
Lightning Source LLC
LaVergne TN
LVHW091225150826
845673LV00003B/1010
9798832780078